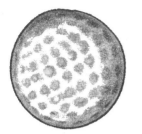

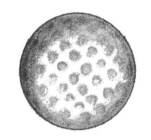

GOLF BUDDIES

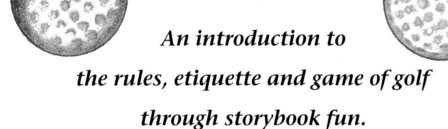

*An introduction to
the rules, etiquette and game of golf
through storybook fun.*

*Written and illustrated
by Susan Martin Mitchell*

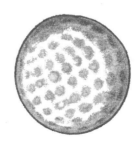

Words in **bold** are defined under
GOLF TERMS & EXPRESSIONS at the end of the book.

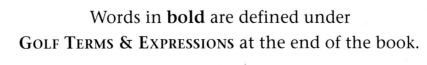
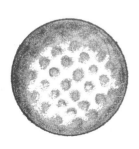

To my grandparents Rhoda and Bob Williams, with whom I spent many happy

days enjoying the beauty of the golf course through the changing seasons.

And to my father, David Martin, who taught me the game of golf and the joy of creativity.

By the same author   DADDY TAKES THE TRAIN TO WORK

ISBN 0-9651598-1-7
Library of Congress Catalog Card Number 97-78229
Printed by Liskey & Sons Printing, Norfolk, VA

Published by:
Busy Buddy Books
P. O. Box 1682
Darien CT 06820
Tel. 1-800-690-9993
Fax (203)852-0271
e-mail: busybuddybooks@juno.com

Busy Buddy Books welcomes your comments and suggestions.

Hello! My name is Buddy and
I'm playing golf today.
Why don't you come along with me?
You'll learn a lot that way!

My Mom will take a lesson while
Dad plays a **round** with me.
He has a **foursome** all lined up—
We'll meet at the first tee!

I see my friends from golf school;
Some are on the **putting green**.
And over on the **driving range**
Are Katie and Kathleen.

For weeks I have been practicing.
At last I get to play!
Dad's **partner** Jack and his son Ted
Will join us for the day.

Ted is a junior golfer and
In summers he's a **caddie**.
I'll watch and try to play like him.
"You'll learn a lot!" says Daddy.

Our **tee time** is at nine o'clock;
We get our clubs and wait.
Oh, hurry! Where are Jack and Ted?
We'll miss it if we're late!

Since I'm a **duffer** I'll go last—
I wait behind the **tee.**
While Dad is **teeing off** I watch
And here is what I see:

Before me is the first hole with its **tee**, **fairway**, and **green**.

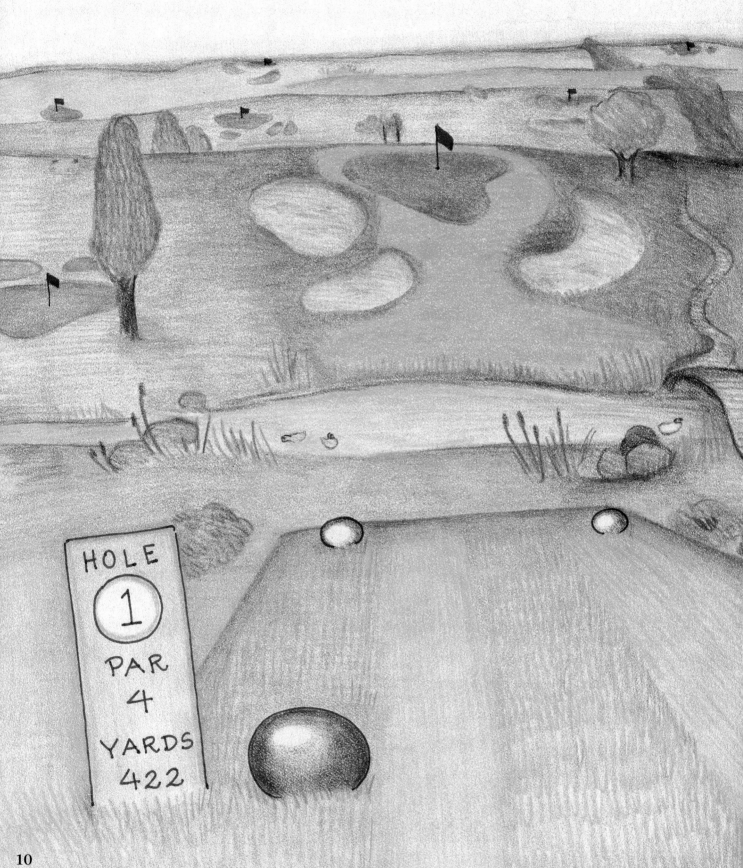

HOLE
1
PAR
4
YARDS
422

I look out over 18 holes, the coolest **course** I've seen.

Can you count 18 holes?

Each hole has challenging **obstacles**

like **hazards**,

traps, and **trees**.

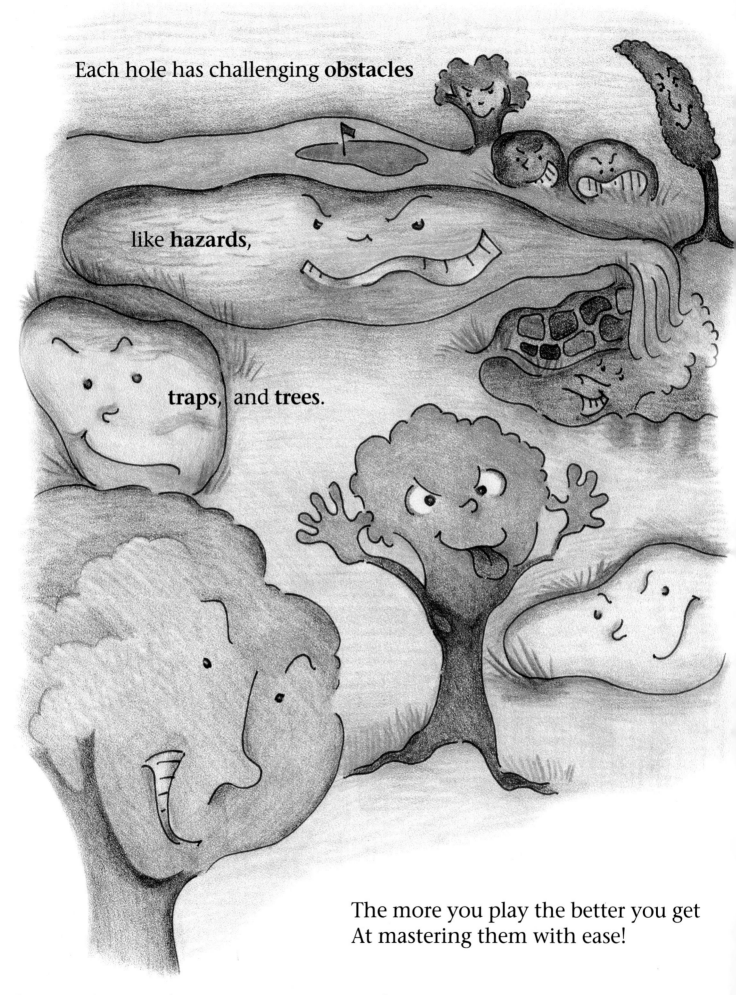

The more you play the better you get
At mastering them with ease!

12

Golf Etiquette

GOLF IS A FUN SPORT AND PLAYERS NEED TO PLAY LIKE LADIES AND GENTLEMEN TO KEEP IT SO.

• BE COURTEOUS ON THE COURSE:
DO NOT MOVE, TALK, OR STAND TOO CLOSE TO A PLAYER MAKING A STROKE. WAIT FOR PLAYERS IN RANGE TO BE OUT OF SIGHT BEFORE HITTING THE BALL. DO NOT DAWDLE!

• GIVE PRIORITY ON THE COURSE:
ALLOW FASTER PLAYERS BEHIND TO PASS.

• TAKE CARE OF THE COURSE:
REPLACE DIVOTS AND BALLMARKS AND SMOOTH BUNKERS. DO NOT DAMAGE THE PUTTING GREEN WITH GOLF BAGS OR PUTTERS. BE A GOOD SPORT!

We watch in silence and respect
As each one takes his turn.
Dad says its called **golf etiquette** —
I've got a lot to learn!

Dad hits the ball with one loud **whack!**
It travels high and far.
He smiles and says he hopes to make
This first hole **under par**.

Jack **hooks** his shot. Ted **slices** his.
The balls fly left and right.
Jack's ball goes in a **bunker** and
Ted's ball rolls out of sight.

The **driver** is the longest **club**,
It hits the ball the farthest.
Some think it is such fun to hit
But I think it's the hardest!

I **whiff** the ball, then **top** the ball,
But I can go again.
The guys will give me one more chance —
It's called a **Mulligan**!

Ted helps me to correct my **stance**;
Jack gives my knees a poke.
Dad shows me how to **follow through**
And swing with one smooth stroke.

Ted helps me grip the club just so—
With right thumb overlapping.
I keep my eye right on the ball
Then swing—Hey! They're all clapping!

My ball does not go very far—
It rolls right near the **rough**.

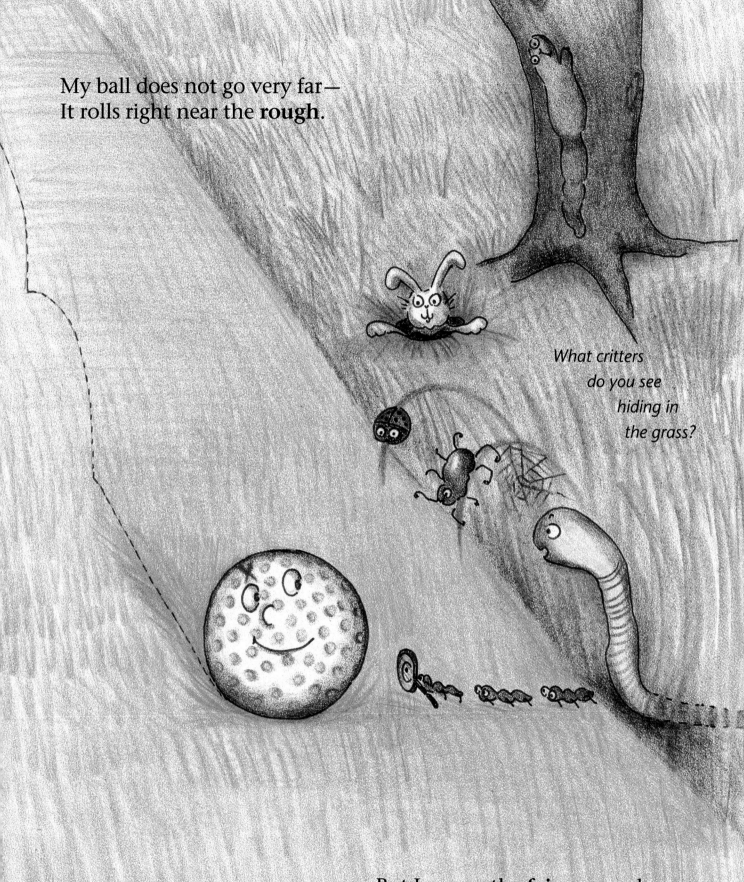

*What critters
do you see
hiding in
the grass?*

But I am on the **fairway** and
For me that's good enough!

"Let's go!" says Ted. "We should move on
Because the next group's ready."
We talk together as we walk.
Let's look for balls with Teddy!

Can you find ten practice balls?

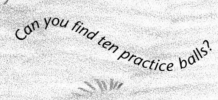

Of course the first ball that we see
Is marked in red—it's mine.
Dad hands a sturdy **iron** to me.
"The five," he says, "is fine."

Basic Set of Clubs

DRIVER   FAIRWAY WOOD (5-WOOD)   5-IRON   7-IRON   PITCHING WEDGE   SAND WEDGE   PUTTER

21

Ahead there is a giant pond.
Watch for the ducks. Quack Quack!
But sure enough, I swing and **splash**.
"You've lost your ball!" says Jack.

"**A water hazard**," Dad explains,
"Is just how this game goes.
You lose a stroke but that's okay!
It happens to the **pros**."

I drop my ball to try again.
I swing, and as I pivot,

My club picks up a clump of dirt.
I must replace my **divot**!

In two more strokes I'm near the green.
I want the ball to roll.
I **chip** it up onto the green—
It stops short of the hole!

chip shot...chip shot...chip shot

Jack's ball is in the bunker
So he'll use his **sand wedge** here.
His club scoops sand up as he swings.
The ball flies free and clear!

Ted's ball has dropped behind the green.
A **pitch shot** is the call.
He lofts the ball up over the hill.
It hardly rolls at all!

pitch shot...pitch shot...pitch shot

"I need my **Texas wedge!**" laughs Dad.
He really means his putter.
"I'll putt from here just off the green;
The grass is smooth as butter!"

Once on the green we take our time
For every shot is key.

A six-inch putt counts just as much
As a **long drive** off the tee.

Take time to read the **contour**—
Where the green goes down and up.
The ball will **break** accordingly
As it rolls toward the **cup**!

I stand with eyes above the ball.
I bend my knees, and then
My arms swing like a **pendulum**.
The ball rolls gently in!

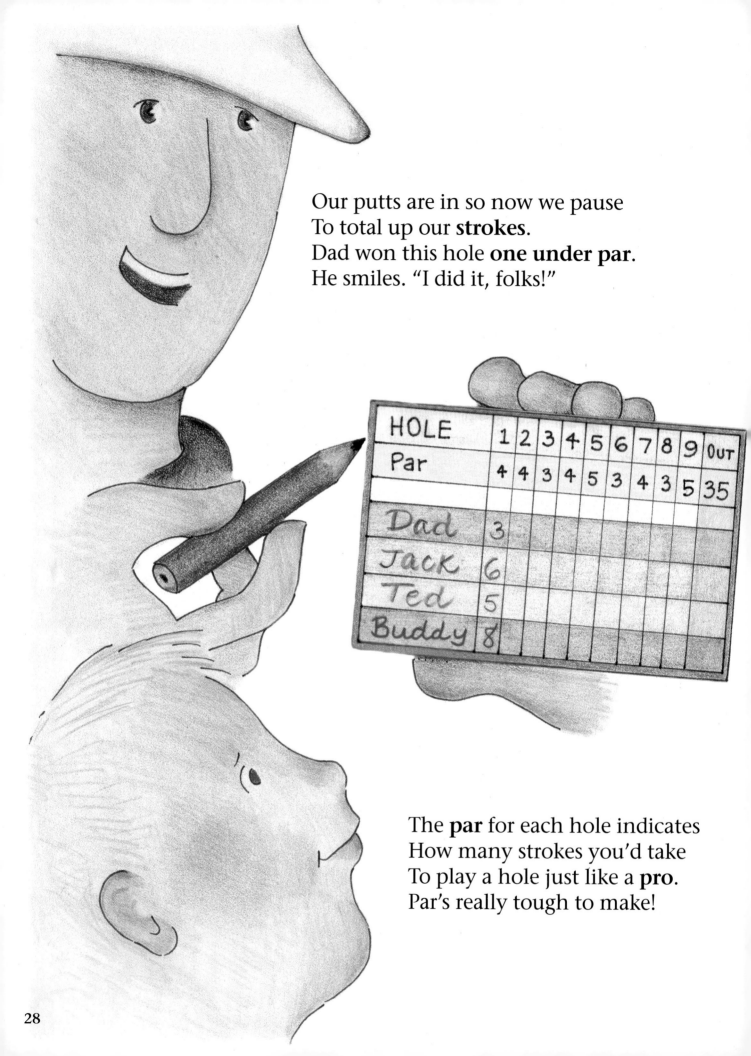

Our putts are in so now we pause
To total up our **strokes**.
Dad won this hole **one under par**.
He smiles. "I did it, folks!"

HOLE	1	2	3	4	5	6	7	8	9	OUT
Par	4	4	3	4	5	3	4	3	5	35
Dad	3									
Jack	6									
Ted	5									
Buddy	8									

The **par** for each hole indicates
How many strokes you'd take
To play a hole just like a **pro**.
Par's really tough to make!

A **birdie** is *one under par.*

Two under par, an **eagle.**

Three under par's an **albatross.**

(Now what would be a sea gull?!)

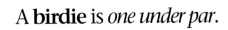

-3	-2	-1	PAR IF PAR IS:	+1	+2	+3
A L B A T R O S S	E A G L E	B I R D I E		B O G E Y	D O U B L E B O G E Y	T R I P L E B O G E Y
—	1	2	3	4	5	6
1	2	3	4	5	6	7
2	3	4	5	6	7	8

A **bogey** is *one over par.*

A **double-bogey,** *two.*

A **triple bogey,** *par plus three.*

Past that, a lesson's due!

A <u>lower</u> score is better !

29

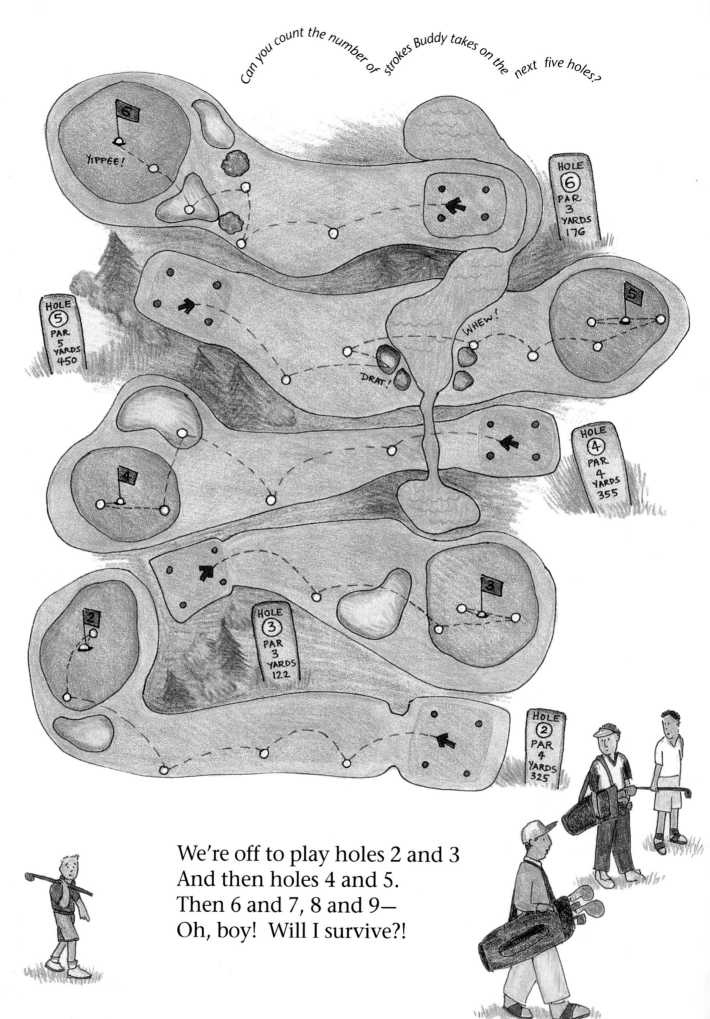

We're off to play holes 2 and 3
And then holes 4 and 5.
Then 6 and 7, 8 and 9—
Oh, boy! Will I survive?!

The 9th hole is our midway point;
We stop to drink some water.
Dad says to rest our feet awhile;
The **back nine's** even harder!

The group behind approaches us.
It's Megan and her Mom.
"Though we're just two, may we **play through**?"
"Of course!" we wave. "Play on!"

I watch as Megan tees off.
Wow! Her ball lands near the **pin**!

"Hey, Meg," I call,
"You nailed that shot.
Now **sink** your putt!" I grin.

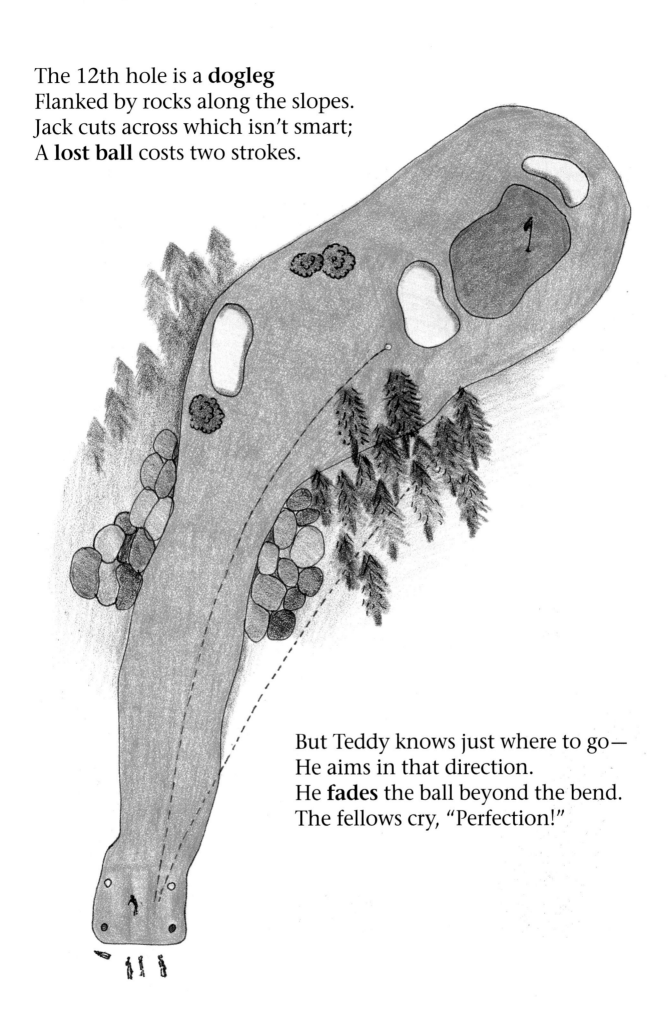

The 12th hole is a **dogleg**
Flanked by rocks along the slopes.
Jack cuts across which isn't smart;
A **lost ball** costs two strokes.

But Teddy knows just where to go—
He aims in that direction.
He **fades** the ball beyond the bend.
The fellows cry, "Perfection!"

Can you find the flying ball?

At hole 15 someone cries "**Fore**!" to warn a ball's in flight.
We want to stay out of its way. The ball flies out of sight.

At last we play the 18th hole
And tally up our strokes.
The fellows clean their balls and clubs
And swap a few golf jokes.

Ted shows me how the **handicap**
Allows someone like me
To play a game with anyone
Despite ability.

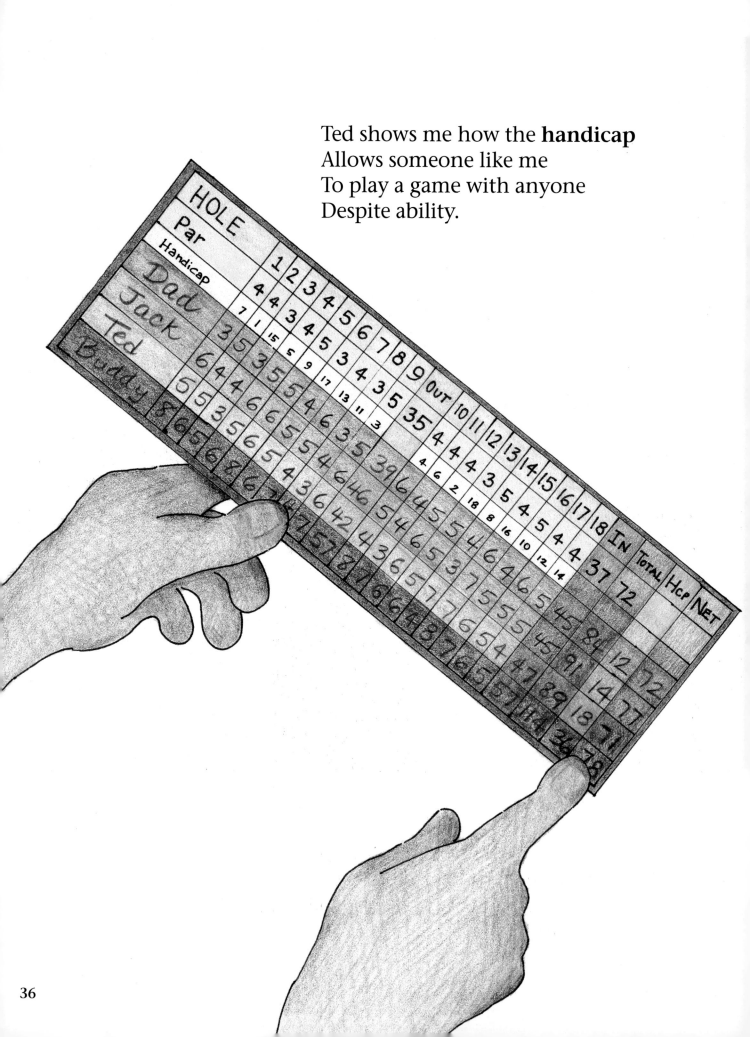

The **19th hole's** a lively place
Where all the golfers meet.
We watch the **Masters** on T.V.
And grab a bite to eat.

I've learned an awful lot today
And had a lot of fun.
Tonight I'll dream that I turned pro
And made a **hole-in-one**!

GOLF TERMS & EXPRESSIONS

Albatross A score of three strokes less than par. Also known as a double-eagle.

Amateur A golfer who competes in tournaments but not for prize money.

Back Nine Second set of nine holes on an 18-hole golf course.

Birdie A score of one stroke less than par.

Bogey A score of one stroke more than par.

Break The point at which a rolling ball changes direction on the green because of changing contours.

Bunker Sand trap.

Caddie Someone hired to carry bags and give advice during a golf game. Caddying is a good way for a young person to learn golf and earn money at the same time.

Chip A shot that travels low to the ground with a lot of bounce. Normally used to get onto the green.

Club The stick used to hit the ball.

Contour The landscape of the green.

Course The large expanse of grass which includes all tees, fairways, greens, hazards, etc., and normally consists of 18 holes.

Cup Small, round hole. The object of golf is to get the ball into the cup in as few strokes as possible.

Divot A clump of dirt knocked out of the ground by a club when making a shot. It is golf etiquette to return a divot to its original spot and press it firmly into place.

Dogleg Hole with a fairway that curves left or right.

Driver The biggest wood, "Number 1." If used effectively, it will hit the ball farther than any other club.

Driving Range An area set aside for practicing shots with woods or irons.

Duffer Beginning or unskilled golfer.

Eagle A score of two strokes less than par.

Etiquette Proper rules of play and sportsmanship.

Fade To purposefully hit the ball so that it moves from left to right while in flight.

Fairway The mown portion of each hole on a golf course between tee and green. The best area for play because the grass is smooth and the ball's line is normally unobstructed.

Follow Through When swinging, to continue through to the natural finish.

Fore The word used to warn that a flying ball is close by and could hit someone. If you hear "Fore," be sure to look for the ball or duck behind a safe barrier.

Foursome A group of four players. No more than four golfers can play together at one time.

Green Putting surface where the grass is cut very short and where you will find the cup (hole) and flagstick (pin).

Handicap A player's average number of strokes he normally hits over par, which he can deduct from the final score. A beginning golfer is often allowed a handicap of two strokes per hole, or a handicap of 36.

Hole Another word for cup. Also, the entire playing area of a "hole" to include the tee, fairway and green.

Hole-in-One To hit the ball from the tee to the cup in one shot. Be sure someone sees you if you ever make one. Otherwise, it's not recorded as having happened!

Hook A shot that curves to the left.

Iron Any club except the putter or wood.

Lost Ball A ball that cannot be found if lost in play or out of bounds. The penalty is *stroke and distance* (the ball must be hit from where it was originally played under a one-stroke penalty).

Masters Professional golf tournament held each year at a private club in Augusta GA. The winner receives a green jacket!

Mulligan "Second chance" shot at tee off offered by competing players if a player's first shot was not good. Not used in serious play.

19th Hole Nickname for the place to relax after finishing the 18th hole.

Obstacle A rock, tree, or other natural obstruction that makes play more difficult if your ball lands near, behind, or in it.

Par The assigned number of strokes for a hole based on its length and allowing for two strokes once on the green. **Par 3** means that a good golfer should be able to hit the ball to the green in one stroke and putt two times into the cup. **Par 4** would allow for two strokes to the green, two strokes into the cup. **Par 5** would allow for three strokes to the green, two strokes into the cup.

Partner A player on the same team.

Pendulum Term used to describe how the arms should be when putting: swinging relaxed but straight down from the shoulders.

Pin The flagstick.

Pitch A high, arching shot that does not bounce much on landing. Normally used to get onto the green.

Play Through The term for allowing players playing behind a slower group to pass.

Practice, Practice Practice The best way to become a better golfer!

Pro Short term for professional golfer. Pros compete for money or work as instructors or coaches.

Putt To hit the ball on the green. A putter, with its flat clubface, is used to tap the ball.

Putting Green A practice green with several cups to practice putts at varying distances.

Rough The grassy area along each side of the fairway that consists of uncut or scruffy grass. It is more difficult to play your ball out of the rough than from the fairway.

Round 18 holes, a complete game of golf.

Sand Wedge A club whose face has greater loft, or more tilt to it, which helps to hit the ball out of sand.

Sink a Putt To put a ball into the cup.

Slice A shot that curves to the right.

Stance The placement of your feet in relation to the ball just before swinging. Proper stance can mean a better swing.

Stroke One swing of the club to hit the ball. Your score is the total number of strokes made from tee to cup.

Tee A peg on which the ball rests for a shot from the teeing area. Also, the grassy area from where the first shot is made at each hole.

Tee Time The time assigned for you to tee off at the first hole, thus starting your round of golf.

Tee Off To hit your first shot at the start of each hole.

Texas Wedge To use a putter instead of an iron to hit from off the green onto it.

Top When swinging, to hit only the top of the ball, moving it just a short distance.

Under Par To make a score lower than the par for the hole, something every golfer tries for!

Water Hazard Any lake, pond, stream, etc. If a ball falls in, the player loses a stroke and must take another, dropping a new ball somewhere between where the original shot was made and the water hazard.

Whiff When swinging, to miss the ball completely!

Wood A club with a wooden head used to tee off (with a tee to hold the ball), and on the fairway (a tee is not used in this case). Today's woods are also made of metal or graphite.